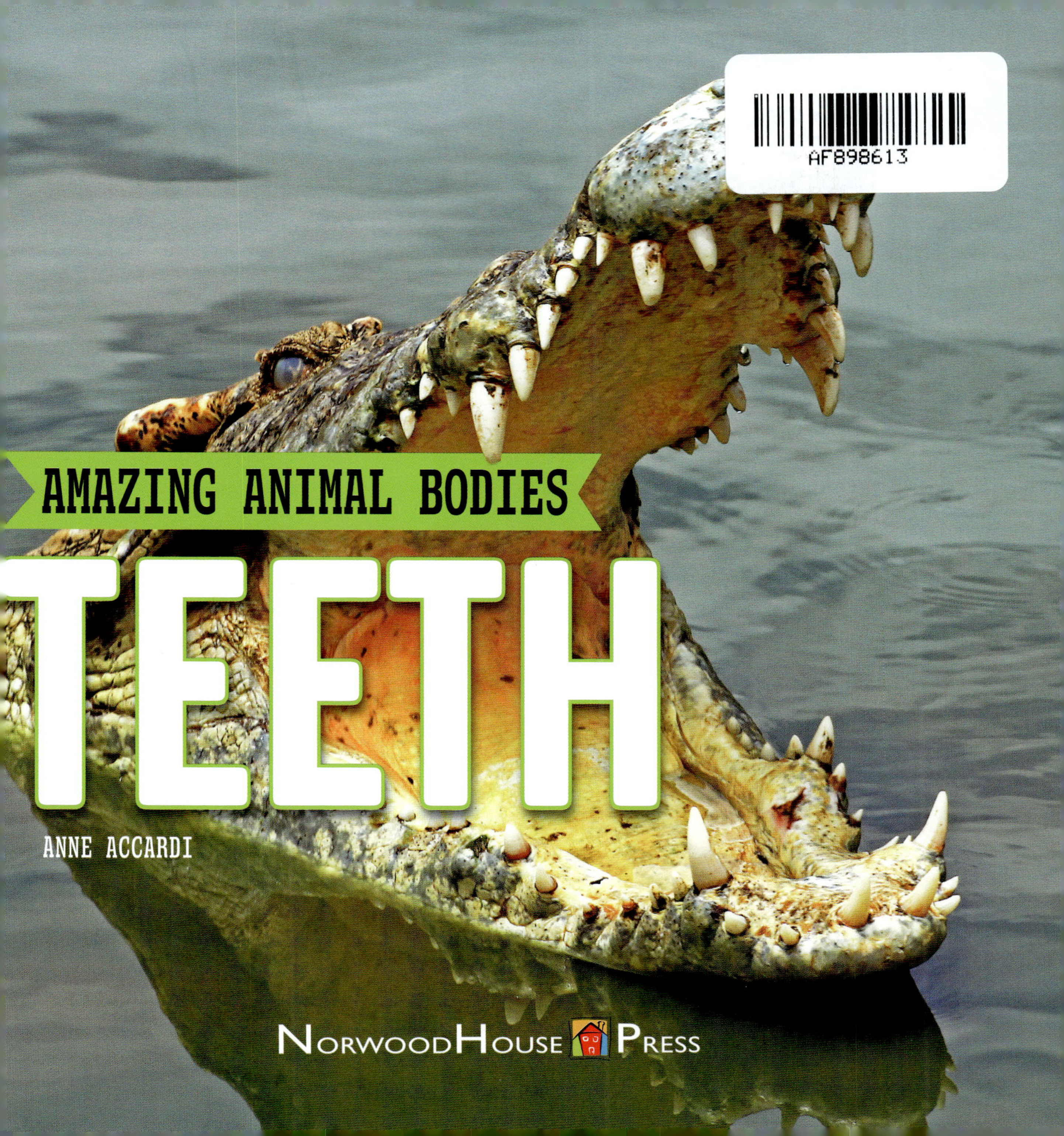

AMAZING ANIMAL BODIES

TEETH

ANNE ACCARDI

NorwoodHouse Press

Cataloging-in-Publication Data

Names: Accardi, Anne.
Title: Teeth / Anne Accardi.
Description: Buffalo, NY : Norwood House Press, 2027. | Series: Amazing animal bodies | Includes glossary and index.
Identifiers: ISBN 9781978579637 (pbk.) | ISBN 9781978579644 (library bound) | ISBN 9781978579651 (ebook)
Subjects: LCSH: Teeth--Juvenile literature. | Animals--Juvenile literature.
Classification: LCC QL858.A33 2027 | DDC 591.44--dc23

Published in 2027 by
Norwood House Press
2544 Clinton Street
Buffalo, NY 14224

Designer: Rhea Magaro
Editor: Kim Thompson

Photo credits: Cover, p. 1 Somluck Rungaree/Shutterstock.com; p. 5 Galovtsik Gabor/Shutterstock.com; p. 6 KM-Photography/Shutterstock.com; p. 7 Eklektyczny_Albert/Shutterstock.com; p. 9 Sourabh Bharti/Shutterstock.com; p. 10 MyImages - Micha/Shutterstock.com; p. 11 Scalia Media/Shutterstock.com; p. 12 Krakenimages.com/Shutterstock.com; p. 14 BlueSnap/Shutterstock.com; p. 15 Marcel Hamonic/Shutterstock.com; p. 17 reptiles4all/Shutterstock.com; p. 18 Alyson W. Kast/Shutterstock.com; p. 21 ChrisVanLennepPhoto/Shutterstock.com;

Printed in the United States of America

CPSIA compliance information: Batch #CSNHP27: For further information contact Norwood House Press at 1-800-237-9932.

TABLE OF CONTENTS

What Are Teeth?

Teeth are strong, hard body parts. They are covered with **enamel**.

Most animals have teeth in their mouths.

Teeth have special jobs.

Canines and **incisors** are sharp. They bite and tear meat.

Molars are flat. They grind and crush plants.

Tiger Teeth

Teeth help tigers hunt. They grab and hold **prey**. They kill with a bite to the neck. They scrape meat from bones.

Beaver Teeth

Beaver teeth contain **iron**. This makes them orange!

Teeth with iron are extra tough. This lets beavers chew wood.

Cat Teeth

A cat uses its front teeth like tiny combs. They smooth fur. They pull out dirt and bugs.

Elephant Teeth

Elephant tusks are very long teeth! They dig and carry. They strip bark from trees for food. Tusks also help elephants protect themselves.

Snake Teeth

Some snakes have special teeth called fangs. They are hollow. **Venom** shoots through them.

Horse Teeth

A horse's teeth never stop growing!

As horses chew, their teeth wear down. This keeps the teeth from getting too long.

Hippo Teeth

Male hippos use their long, strong teeth for fighting.

They battle for **dominance**.

Glossary

canines (KAY-nines): sharp, pointed teeth in the front of the mouth that are used to bite, tear, and rip food

dominance (DAH-muh-nuhns): power and control

enamel (i-NAM-uhl): the hard, white surface of teeth; the strongest part of most animals' bodies

incisors (in-SYE-zurz): sharp front teeth that cut food

iron (EYE-urn): a kind of metal that is found in the body, including in blood

molars (MOH-lurz): wide, flat teeth in the back of the mouth that are used for grinding and crushing food

prey (pray): animals eaten by other animals

venom (VEN-uhm): a poison produced by some snakes and spiders

Thinking Questions

1. Name three kinds of teeth.

2. Describe a beaver's teeth.

3. What are tusks?

4. What are fangs?

5. What keeps a horse's teeth from getting too long?

Index

About the Author

Anne Accardi is a librarian who loves reading books and learning new things! She lives in Kansas City, Missouri. When she's not writing, Anne enjoys listening to music, exploring nature around the city, and spending time with her family.